H(

HOW TO
WIN ON
THE HORSES

by Orry Whitehand

HOW TO WIN ON THE HORSES

Table of Contents

HOW TO WIN ON THE HORSES

Chapter One

What This Book Does and Doesn't Do

Horse racing is an exciting sport to watch, and a race meeting is a real blast to attend. But hand in hand with horse racing has always been the thrill of having a flutter, of placing a bet, then waiting with bated breath to see where your chosen horse is placed at the line.

Many of us enjoy betting, and we all like to win. Who doesn't dream of that elusive accumulator which will net us a fortune, or that 100-1 shot who crosses the line first?

I'm afraid this booklet can't help you with those big wins. There are racing tipsters out there who claim to have inside information and who sell hot tips, and you might consider using the services of one of these if that's your thing. But this book isn't about the long shots, nor does the system I'm going to teach you use accumulators. It's all straight win bets, and it's calculated to bring you a lot of consistent small wins instead of a few big ones.

I'm not claiming that the system in this book is going to make anybody rich. It certainly hasn't made me rich, there are no false promises here. But it is designed to nicely supplement your income on a regular, consistent basis. And if you invest a portion of your winnings back into your betting bank (as suggested later in these pages), it's possible that you could make quite a comfortable living simply through betting on horses.

The system offered here is twofold. It's all based upon maths and statistics and has been extensively used and tested over a period of several years to prove its efficacy and reliability.

It uses a staking plan to determine how much to bet in each instance and to ensure that any losses are recovered in full without impacting on your winnings. And it uses a method for selecting which horse to bet on in a race. It takes just about twenty minutes' work on the evening before the race meeting you're betting on to plan your bets.

This booklet covers the following topics:

- How to Place a Bet
- Your Betting Bank and Profits
- Planning a Sequence of Bets
- Selecting Which Horses to Bet On
- When Not to Bet
- How to Keep Betting

Enjoy the sport and spectacle of the races, which are always more fun when you're winning!

This booklet deals with horse racing and gambling in the UK. There may be slight variations in other countries, especially with tax and such matters, but the general principles should remain the same and be readily adaptable. Where publications such as the *Racing Post* are referenced here, you should substitute racing papers or web sites appropriate to your country.

Chapter Two

How to Place a Bet

It's possible you've never placed a bet before, or have only done so with mates. If so, you may be uncertain about such things as accumulators or 'each way' bets. Don't be. This system only uses straightforward bets for a single named horse to win a specific race.

So when you place your bet, you just write down the name of the race meeting (Goodwood or Thirsk, for example), the time of the race you're betting on, the name of the horse, followed by the words 'to Win'. In some bookmakers' establishments, this may be mostly a matter of ticking boxes, in others they ask you to write it all out yourself. Some of the older gents may write it down for you if you tell them what you want. The main thing is that you want to place a simple bet 'to win'.

Betting is taxable. There is usually the option to pay tax in advance, in which case the percentage is added to the price of your stake; or upon a win, in which case the percentage is deducted from your winnings.

For simplicity's sake, this system assumes that all tax will be paid in advance. The system allows for this when calculating the size of bet to win your target profit (explained later), so it's taken fully into account.

When the race is over, if your horse has won, you collect back your stake money plus your winnings from the bookmaker. If it does not win, you would then place the next bet in your sequence as determined by the system.

There are many options open to punters these days. You can place your bet at your local bookies', or you can use a branch of a national chain of bookmakers. Most of these large firms now have the facility to place bets online also. You could place your bets with bookmakers actually present at the track during the race meeting, or you could have an agent place your bets for you. (This latter option may seem strange, but its usefulness will be explained in due course.) You will probably use all of these options at various times and I'll give a lot more guidance on the use of bookmakers in chapter seven, titled 'How to Keep Betting'.

Chapter Three

Your Betting Bank and Profits

The first question you need to ask yourself when using this system is: "How much do I want to win per race?" Don't be too greedy initially, because your initial winning capacity is limited by the size of your betting bank. Your betting bank is the fund you keep reserved exclusively for placing bets. And you may find yourself running into trouble if you're not disciplined enough to keep it to one side and not dip into it for other things. You can spend your profits, but once you have designated your betting bank, it is no longer available to you for other purchases. If you reduce it while you have bets in play and thus can't cover the next bet in the sequence, you could find yourself losing badly and left unable to recoup your losses. I have seen this happen catastrophically when people have been hit by unexpected expenses and have raided their betting bank, then found they could no longer cover all the races at a meeting and lost the lot in consequence. The reason for this will become clear as we examine the mathematics of the system in the next chapter. Just remember that your betting bank is sacred.

The money you have available to place in your betting bank will initially determine the answer to that crucial first question. Since this system utilises a staking plan to recoup all losses, your bank will need to contain enough money to cope with a potential string of five or six lost bets, each one bigger than those before. And if the odds are short (this will be explained in the next couple of chapters), the bets can get very large.

So my guidance is that your betting bank should be 50 times larger than the amount of money you want to win in each race.

This means that if you want to win £10 per race, you will need to set aside a betting bank of £500; if you want to start smaller and aim for £5 profit per race, you will need only a betting bank of £250.

This may seem excessive to some, but it is better to be safe than sorry. In practice, you will hopefully find that it is a very rare occasion that you come close to using the upper limits of your betting bank. But it can and does happen on rare occasions, and you will need to be prepared for it or risk a heavy loss that you'd simply have to write off. And this system is **not** about making losses! So I'll say it again: make sure your betting bank is large enough to sustain your full sequence of bets, and don't be tempted to dip into it for other purposes.

Managing Your Winnings

When you place your first bet of the day, your betting bank will be nice and full, so you simply take out the

11

money to cover that first bet.

If your horse loses the first race, the process is simple: you calculate the bet required for the next race at that meeting and take that too from the bank and place it on the appropriate horse.

But let's consider what happens when you get your winner. To keep the sums simple, we'll assume you placed a £5 bet on a horse at 3/1 odds. This means that for every £1 you bet, you will receive back £3 if that horse wins the race: the second number in the odds figure is the amount wagered; the first number is the proportionate amount won.

If this bet is a winner, you will receive £20 back from the bookmaker: £5 of this is your stake money, which should be returned to your betting bank! The other £15 is your profit. Never forget to separate your stake from your winnings and return it to your betting bank.

Now it's up to you what you do with your profit. You can spend it on anything at all if you like. But if you'll take a tip from an old pro, you'll consider setting aside half of your profits until you've saved up enough money to have a second betting bank. The other half is yours to do with as you please, of course.

Why do I advise you to set aside enough money to form a second betting bank? This system is pretty foolproof and has all manner of safeguards built in (provided you follow all the advice given in this booklet, of course!), but nothing is ever 100% guaranteed and watertight. It may not be likely, but there's always a remote chance that you may hit a really bad losing streak and lose your entire betting bank. It shouldn't happen, but it's not impossible.

If you have set aside a second betting bank from

your winnings (something that it will take you surprisingly little time to do), you can just philosophically shrug the loss off and start anew with the second bank. And from **its** winnings, you can then set half aside to establish a new reserve bank, covering yourself once again.

In this manner, you'll be able to resume betting and it won't have cost you a penny, because the money which has gone into forming the replacement bank is money you set aside from your profits (half of which you have already pocketed), so effectively it's money you've never even had, you're not having to fork out anything extra. You haven't really lost anything at all. This is a hugely important safety net which gives great peace of mind, and I strongly urge you to do it.

Once you have put aside enough from your winnings to create a second bank, you can then pocket all your profits from that point on, of course. Enjoy them! Or, you could keep putting a little aside, to gradually increase the size of your banks. By doing this, you will be able to gradually increase the target amount you aim to win from each race. And again, you're doing this and increasing your earning potential by reinvesting a percentage of your profits, not by pumping in fresh capital, so you're risking nothing. It makes sense.

Chapter Four

Planning a Sequence of Bets

In the next chapter, we'll discuss how to select which bets to place, but first let's take a look how to calculate a day's sequence of bets, working out how much money to bet on each race and when to stop.

However you choose to place your bets, whether at a local bookmaker, online, or by telephone, you should sit down and do all of your calculations for the day first. This can be done in about twenty minutes when you're familiar with the process. You might choose to sit down and do it over breakfast whilst reading the *Racing Post*, or you might choose to work it all out the previous evening, by looking up the next day's race cards on the *Racing Post*'s website.[1]

You will be calculating bets for all races to be held at one specific race meeting on that day. For

---

1   Substitute a racing paper or website local to yourself if outside the British Isles.

example, looking at the *Racing Post*'s website[2] for Friday 24th April 2015, I can see that there are race meetings at Chepstow, Doncaster, Perth, Plumpton and Sandown in the UK.

If we select Chepstow as an example, and choose to be bet on the Favourites, we find the following horses running at the following odds:

Time	Horse	Odds
5.05	Risk a Fine	6/4
5.35	Mr Burbidge	9/4
6.05	Brody Bleu	15/8
6.35	Modeligo	4/1
7.10	Desertmore View	5/4
7.40	Charming Lad	9/4
8.10	Bringithomeminty	Evens

We'll assume that we have available a £500 betting bank and are aiming to win £10 for every race we bet on. I will discount the final race, because most race meetings have six rather than seven races and the betting bank is geared toward a maximum of six consecutive bets (unless, of course, you wish to increase the 'gearing' of the bank to 60 or 70 times your desired profit instead of 50 times).

The formula for calculating the bet for the first race is easy:

Target Profit + Tax[3], adjusted by Odds = Amount to Bet

------

2   www.racingpost.com
3   assumed to be 10%

which becomes:

10.00 + 10% = 11.00 ÷ 6 X 4^4 = 7.33

This means that the amount you will need to bet on Risk a Fine in the 5.05 race to win £10 profit is £7.33. In practice, most bookmakers prefer bets for round amounts and some online bookies have minimum bets of £10 or £20. So round the amount of to £8 (if using a local bookie), or £10 (if online). For our example, we'll assume you're using a local bookmaker who will be happy to accept an £8 bet.

     If your bet wins, by these odds you'll get back £6 for every £4 bet. So in this case, you would receive back your £8 stake, plus £12 profit, for a total of £20. The £8 stake money would be returned to your betting bank, you have your intended £10 profit, plus another £1 rebating the tax paid on the bet, plus an extra £1 since you rounded the bet up.

     If Risk a Fine lost his race, however, and you lost your bet in consequence, you would then proceed to bet on the second race at the meeting. But in this case, your target profit would increase from £10 to £20, because you want to win £10 for **every** race you bet on; even though your bet on the first race may have lost, you still want your profit on it, so it gets added to the second bet's target profit. Also, you need to recover the money you lost when your horse lost the first race.

     So the formula for your second bet becomes:

---

4   To calculate the adjustment for the odds, divide by the number to the left of the stroke, then multiply by the number to the right.

Target Profit + Accumulated Losses + Tax, adjusted by Odds = Amount to Bet

Our second bet is on Mr Burbidge in the 5.35 race at 9/4 odds, so this works out as follows:

20.00 + 8.00 + 10% = 30.80 ÷ 9 X 4 = 13.69

This means that the second bet will be £13.69, best rounded up to £15.00.

If this bet wins, you would receive back £33.75 profit, plus the return of your £15 stake. This £33.75 would give you your target profit (£20), the money you had lost with your first bet (£8), the tax paid (£2.80), plus an extra £2.95 since you rounded the bet up.

If the second bet is also a loser, you would proceed to the third, using the same formula. This time your target profit would be £30, since this would be the third bet in the sequence, and you would want to recoup your losses from both the previous bets (£8 + £15 = £23). So the third bet at 15/8 odds would look like this:

30.00 + 23.00 + 10% = 58.30 ÷ 15 X 8 = 31.09

The bet would therefore be rounded up to £32 or £35.

If you are actually at the track, or sitting in the bookmaker's shop, you may have the luxury of calculating each bet as you place it. But to keep things easy, it's always a good idea to calculate the entire race card in advance, working out what each bet will be if you lose the ones before (because this plan continues through the card until you reach a winner). Each time, the target profit increases by one increment, and the

17

losses to be recouped from previous bets are added together. The remaining four bets at our sample race meeting at Chepstow would therefore work out like this:

6.35 Modeligo at 4/1 odds:

40.00 + 55.00 + 10% = 104.50 ÷ 4 X 1 = 26.13 (£28)

7.10 Desertmore View at 5/4 odds:

50.00 + 83.00 + 10% = 146.30 ÷ 5 X 4 = 117.04 (£120)

7.40 Charming Lad at 9/4 odds:

60.00 + 203.00 + 10% = 289.30 ÷ 9 X 4 = 128.58 (£130)

So if the betting went as far as the sixth race in the sequence, you would have bet a total of £333 on this day, well within the betting bank's reach. As stated earlier the final, seventh race is discounted because the bank is geared towards covering the first six races at a meeting.

The actual winners of these six races were as follows:

5.05	Anteros	13/8
5.35	Mr Burbidge	9/4
6.05	Brody Bleu	15/8
6.35	Ballyknock Lad	14/1
7.10	Desertmore View	9/4
7.40	Charming Lad	9/4

So it can be seen that we would have bet on the correct horse in four of the six races. This would have been a particularly good day, as we only needed a single winner.

This staking system stops when you reach a winner. So if your first choice horse wins, you would stop after the very first race. You keep on betting, moving down the race card, calculating each bet, until one of your horses wins its race. At this point, you will win your target profit for the number of races you bet on, plus enough to cover the betting tax, plus any losses from previous bets. You don't continue betting that day after you have scored a winner.

This is easy to do if you are in a bookmaker's or at the track, or placing bets online as the results come in. But it gets more difficult if you are at work that day and can't keep track of the results or place your bets immediately you need to. If that is the case. you will need to restrict your betting to your days off work.

The alternative is to use an agency to place your bets for you. Look in adverts in the racing press or online. In these cases, you would lodge your betting bank with the agency and would telephone them each day to list your bets. You could tell them the bets you have calculated for the entire race card as explained above, then instruct them to "stop at a winner". They would follow your instructions precisely. At regular intervals, they will provide a statement of your account and pay you your profits.

Of course, an agency will charge a commission, but this can be easily allowed for by increasing the tax percentage allowance in the bet calculation to include their commission too.

There are other very great advantages in betting through an agency, which will be discussed in chapter seven.

Some bookmakers may also offer a service whereby they will accept a sequence of bets with an instruction to "stop at a winner". But for reasons also explained in chapter seven, this will inevitably be a short term solution.

Chapter Five

Selecting Which Horses to Bet On

So now you now how to calculate your bets, but this still raises the question: which horses should you bet on? Quite a few people use staking plans of one kind or another to plan their bets (after much practice and adjustment, the one in the previous chapter is the best such plan I have encountered). But there's very little point in having a betting bank sufficient to cover six bets if you're going to bet on six losers.

So as well as a plan to maximise profits and recoup any losses, it's essential to bet on horses which are likely to win.

Over the years I have used a large number of different methods to identify likely winners. For a long time, I used a computer program called *Pro-Punter*. This software requires you to input a lot of data, which it then analyses to predict the likely winner of a race. It worked very well and if you want to really immerse yourself in the world of horse racing it's kind of fun too.

It certainly beats any racing tipsters and as well as highlighting obvious winners, it also successfully identified some long shots with great odds on several occasions.

I don't use the software now, but I can still recommend it for anyone who really wants to delve into racing as a fun sport to follow instead of just an earning strategy. They appear to have updated software packages available at http://www.pro-punter-package.co.uk/ and are worth a look if you'd like to use your computer to assist your betting. The tone of the web page is a bit too messianic, but that's marketing for you, I guess!

I then used a really quick system of calculating winners that I found in a book by a professional punter. Sadly, the book is long since lost and I can't remember either the title or author. Given that this was over 20 years ago, it's probably no longer in print anyway, but similar systems are out there. It relied on giving simple number scores to each horse based upon a number of factors (weight, ground, past wins, trainer's wins, etc.) To my surprise, this simple calculation proved equally, if not more, effective than the software.

But it's not either of those systems that I want to share with you in this booklet. They were both good, I can recommend them both. But after years of betting and research, the most reliable system I have come to use is laughable in its simplicity. It will save you a lot of time and produce the winners you need.

Quite simply, I bet on the favourites.

Some of you may be throwing your hands over your heads in dismay now, saying things like "Only losers bet on the favourites" or "The odds for favourites are so poor". But this is missing the point. The odds for favourites are low because favourites win races. And with our staking plan, it doesn't matter if the odds aren't 20/1 or 33/1, because the bet amount is adjusted to win a specified target profit. So this protestation is simply irrelevant.

After trawling through reams and reams of race cards and results, it became blindingly obvious that at any given race meeting, an average of two out of six races will be won by the favourites. Sometimes (as in the case of our sample race card at Chepstow in chapter four where four favourites won) it will be more. Occasionally only one favourite may win. But the occasions when no favourites win any of the races at a meeting are very rare indeed. The rare exceptions to this rule will be highlighted in the next chapter, which will discuss the warning signs which will tell you when not to bet.

It stands to reason. If favourites didn't win this frequently, punters would get angry and bookmakers would face problems as their books would be unbalanced if a sufficient number of people didn't bet on the horses with shorter odds. The whole betting game is a finely balanced machine, relying on the statistics remaining constant for both punters and bookmakers.

Most people who bet on favourites are casual betters, who are satisfied with their occasional small wins. We are taking advantage of these predictable statistics to engage in a series of bets designed to return a specific profit. The staking plan and the selection of favourites go hand in hand to create a money-making machine.

It's not quite as simple as betting on all favourites in every race, of course. Let's follow the process through, looking at race meetings on Monday 27 April

2015 in the UK.

As I refer to the *Racing Post* website, I can see that there are race meetings today at Ayr, Kempton, Southwell, Windsor and Wolverhampton.

I'll now call up the race cards for each of these meetings. As explained in the previous chapter, we will select only **one** of these meetings to bet on and will then calculate bets for the first **six** races at that meeting.

So how do I select which race meeting to bet on? What criteria am I looking at?

We want to look for the meeting which is the most 'average' out of the bunch. If you choose a meeting where the racers have too many runners, it increases the number of variables, which makes things less predictable. So don't go selecting the Grand National or Royal Ascot, select something more middling. If you select a race meeting where all the horses in each race have long odds, 5/1 or greater, then it increases uncertainty. But if you select a meeting where the favourites' odds are **too** short (evens, 8/15 or worse), then your bets will get far too big too quickly, emptying your betting bank too fast. Ideally, you are looking at a meeting where the average favourite's odds are between 2/1 and 4/1.

That's an ideal, of course. Most times, you might find that the closest meeting to this ideal still has at least one race where you'll need to bet on short odds. If that's the case, try to choose one where the short odds are in one of the earlier races. It's easier to cover a short bet when the stake is still low, than when you're trying to hit a hiked profit and recoup prior losses.

So bearing these guidelines in mind, let's have a look at the race cards for these five meetings. I'll list the favourites for each race according to the website below.

24

AYR

1.50	Spirit of Wedza	2/1
2.25	Indego Blues	3/1
3.00	Roy's Legacy	7/2
3.30	Al Khan	11/4
4.05	Sakhalin Star	5/2
4.35	Argaki	11/4

KEMPTON

1.40	Black Key	11/4
2.15	Acaster Malbis	11/4
2.50	Cloud Seven	6/1
3.20	Squire	9/2
3.55	Light Rose	7/2
4.25	Able Dash	9/4

SOUTHWELL

1.30	Marciano	3/1
2.05	La Dorotea	1/2
2.40	Lizzy's Dream	100/30
3.10	Reflektor	5/2
3.45	Sparkling Sapphire	2/1
4.15	Moon Over Rio	11/4

WINDSOR

5.30	Shanghai Glory	9/4
6.00	Gossiping	2/1
6.30	Wonder Laish	6/4
7.00	Arc Lighter	9/4

| 7.30 | Light of Asia | 100/30 |
| 8.00 | Calendula | 4/1 |

WOLVERHAMPTON

6.20	Schottische	11/4
6.50	Lady Atlas	11/4
7.20	Mighty Zip	5/2
7.50	Crazy Chic	11/4
8.20	Black Truffle	4/1
8.50	Scooner	2/1

None of these are bad race cards. Up against other company, any of these would be worth taking a punt on. But we need to narrow it down to a single meeting. Looking at our guidelines, I'm going to discount Southwell, because it's the only race meeting with a favourite with odds poorer than evens. I'm also discounting Kempton, because at 6/1 one of its bets would be longer odds than generally preferred. Of the remaining three, I'm plumping for Windsor, because its races have slightly fewer runners than the other two. There's not much in it and they all look like promising prospects, but we need to decide on one somehow, so Windsor it is.

The results for the six races at Windsor were as follows:

5.30	Silver Wings	7/2
6.00	Gossiping	5/4
6.30	Richard of Yorke	14/1
7.00	Croquembouche	4/1
7.30	All Talk N No Do	7/2
8.00	Stolen Story	12/1

As can be seen, we had a winner here with Gossiping in the second race. The odds have shrunk a bit from the *Racing Post*'s estimate, but this would be remedied by either placing the bet at fixed odds instead of starting price (always best practice), or if it **was** placed at the starting price, the slight shortfall could be made up by adding it onto the first of tomorrow's bets as if it was a loss to be recouped.

For the record, one favourite won at Ayr, one at Kempton, two at Southwell and three at Wolverhampton. So every race meeting on this day would have validated the system and furnished a profit.

So how do you identify the favourite in a race? It is the horse with the shortest odds. It is usually helpfully marked for you with a letter 'F' after its price to indicate that it is the current favourite to win the race (for example, 6/4F). These odds will be displayed at the bookmaker's or frequently displayed on the television screen if you're following a race meeting that way.

The *Racing Post* displays its anticipated prices for each horse at the foot of each race card the evening before the race, and these are generally very accurate so you can make your calculations based upon them. These are available for all to see from 9am on the race day, but they are viewable by subscribers to their Members' Club the evening before the race. Club members are also able to view the paper's spotlight verdict online on the day of the race, so it's worth considering. You can then prepare your bets in a leisurely manner the evening before and you can read the paper's verdict to help you decide which race meeting to choose.

Final determination of favourites may sometimes

fluctuate before a race, but I generally stick with the *Racing Post*'s choice and try to place the bet with fixed odds.

Chapter Six

When Not to Bet

We've worked out a system to decide which horses to bet on, and how much to bet. But are there ever times when we should decide that discretion is the better part of valour and refrain from betting?

Of course there are, and in this chapter I'll try to highlight some of the things to be wary of.

The first big no-no is major race meetings. Where you get a huge race, such as the Grand National, with a lot of runners and major media interest, avoid it. I'm sure all UK readers of this booklet will have watched the Grand National on television at one point or another, and overseas readers will be familiar with their own major races. There are so many horses in the field that too many random factors come into play. Horses are more likely to be nervous and refuse to run in such an atmosphere; there's more scope for accidents; simply more room all round for 101 unforeseen little hiccups to occur. By all means, have a flutter on a big race just for the fun of it if you want to, but don't take the stake from your betting bank and don't select such a high profile meeting for your daily betting.

Try to avoid betting on meetings where the favourites have particularly short odds. If three or four of the horses have odds which are poorer than 2/1, your bets are going to get very large very quickly and will probably empty your betting bank. You should take it as an **absolute rule** that if the odds are too low to allow you to bet on six consecutive races, do not bet at all. It may be disappointing to have to wait a day without betting, but it's better than losing your bank.

On the other hand, if the odds are all longer than usual, do not bet on that meeting. If more than 2 horses have odds longer than 4/1, forget it. That means there is too much uncertainty about the favourites.

You can usually write off one or two race meetings for these reasons each day when you make your selection. But very occasionally, you may find that all of the meetings on a particular day fall foul of these guidelines. Do **not** be tempted, but postpone betting till the next day's meetings.

You should also be very wary at the commencement of each new racing season. At these times, there has been no recent form for any of the horses, so the initial odds are more guesswork than science. There also tend to be a lot of novice races at such times. These horses have never been formally raced before, so the determination of their odds is very speculative. So if the flat season is just beginning, try to restrict your betting to the closing races of the jumps season as the two overlap. And vice versa when the seasons change again. There may be quite a few days at season changes when you feel understandably cautious and shouldn't place bets. Better to be cautious than to lose your betting bank. This system depends upon predictability, so be very wary of chance elements.

The golden rule is: **if in any doubt at all, don't bet!**

Chapter Seven

How to Keep Betting

You might be scratching your head at the title of this chapter and saying, "Surely all I need to do is keep following the system and placing bets?" Sadly, it's not as simple as that.

When I first started using this system some 25 years ago, I opened a credit account with my local bookies. Three weeks later, my account was closed and his staff were instructed to accept no more of my bets.

Contrary to what you might expect, bookmakers love winners. When other punters see someone else win and perhaps showing great delight about it, it makes them think that they can win too, so they're more likely to place more bets. Winners are great for bookies' business!

This, after all, is how bookies balance their books. They take bets on all horses in a race, adjusting the odds so that whichever horse wins, they make enough money from the bets on the others to make a profit overall. So they're winning even as they pay out.

But someone who consistently wins is bad for business, because this is obviously someone who's going to be taking more from the bookmaker than he pays in, and he's going to keep on doing so unless he's stopped. And under current legislation, a bookmaker is perfectly within his rights to refuse an account and to refuse a bet. So if he decides you're costing him too much money, he'll snuff out your opportunity to bet, just as simple as that. When that happens, there's no point in complaining, you just have to move on.

Back in those early days, I was placing all of my bets through that same local bookie, so after a week or two, it became blindingly obvious to him what I was doing. I had an account and I was able to collect a nice pot of winnings three weeks on the trot. What probably rubbed salt in the wound was the fact that it was a credit account, so I was basically using his own money to win from him, I'd never handed over so much as a penny, I just kept taking. As I collected that third week's winnings, his shop manager made it clear to me that the game was up.

A few weeks later, I was placing my bets by physically going to the bookies' shop in a nearby town. I was self-employed at the time, so used to spend my mornings and evenings working and the afternoon betting. Here too I was rapidly identified as someone who consistently left the shop with more money than I had entered it with. This manager was more subtle about it, though. Having realised that I was using a staking plan of some description, he started limiting the size of my bets. If I calculated that I needed to place a bet for £20, he would look at me and say, "I'll take £10". In this way, I was unable to run the system and recoup losses, so he effectively closed me down.

A short while later, I lodged my betting bank with the Track Betting Agency in Sussex. This meant a commission was payable on each bet, but my bets would never be refused. Agents collect bets from a large number of people, then place some bets at the track and others in a broad span of bookmakers' shops. Since they're generally betting large amounts on behalf of several clients across the entire race card, they don't get turned away. Some of these bets will win and others will lose, but the bookmakers never know who the original punter is. This is by far the best way I have found to get your bets placed, and the agency will also accept a single phone call listing the entire day's bets, along with an instruction to "stop at a winner". I simply had to calculate my bets from the paper in the morning (this was in pre-internet days), make my call and then check the results on teletext in the evening.

After a time, when starting a new job and moving home, I stopped betting for a while. I believe Track Betting Agency has long since closed its doors, but there will be others out there and they should be considered.

For now, the internet has made life so much easier. There are a lot of online bookmakers. The 'big boys', such as William Hill, Ladbrokes and Coral all have direct links on the *Racing Post* website to place bets, but there are plenty of others too. This means that you can sit at your laptop, get instant notice of results, and place your next bet at a **different** online bookmaker. If you keep moving between them from one bet to the next, they're not going to notice the pattern of your staking plan and their suspicions won't be aroused. This is probably the easiest, most hassle free approach to betting on horses with a plan such as this one in the modern world. So far, I've experienced no troubles at all. And with the relatively small size of bets generated by this system, no unfavourable attention is likely to be drawn. It's all a matter of scale, as these guys are dealing with huge amounts of money on every race. So online betting is my best recommendation for you, at least when starting out

That question of scale brings us to the last consideration, though. This system is designed to operate with a betting bank of around £500 for best results, aiming at a profit of £10 per race, perhaps building to a bank of £1,500 with a profit of £30 per race.

You may wonder why you can't keep increasing your betting bank indefinitely. After all, if you keep putting aside half your profits as I suggested and reinvesting in the bank, as your target profit increases, the bank will increase exponentially. Why, before you know it you could be winning thousands of pounds on every race!

Don't do it.

The most important advice I can give you here is don't be greedy. Build up your bank and your reserve bank till they reach £1,500 each, aim for a maximum of £30 profit per race, and when you've built up to that, simply pocket all your profits and enjoy them. Don't overreach yourself.

This plan isn't intended to produce millionaires, it's intended to supplement your income. If you bet six days per week and build your target profit up to £30 per race, you're likely to be pocketing somewhere around £360 per week from this plan at its height. That's not to be sniffed at for the small amount of work involved. Stick to this and you'll likely stay below the radar and be able to continue indefinitely.

If you get greedy and start betting hundreds, you'll come to people's attention and they'll take measures to either stop you betting or run interference so you can't stick to the plan.

That being said, have fun and enjoy the extra money that this system can bring to you.

****

Why not spend a little time testing the system out before you commit any money to it? Follow the race cards online, make your calculations as if you were placing the bets, then work out what your winnings would have been. This will familiarise you with the process and give you some confidence when you put it into practice!

Printed in Great Britain
by Amazon